The **Ups** and **Downs** of a
Lockkeeper

Also by Jake Kavanagh:

Worse Things Happen at Sea
ISBN 978-1-4081-1642-5

Worse Things Happen at Sea is the long-awaited
follow-up to Jake Kavanagh's hugely popular
Ups and Downs of a Lockkeeper.

This time turning his humorous eye on the scrapes people
get into when let loose on open water, Jake has us chuckling,
blushing and recognising ourselves (or fellow crew) coming
unstuck in the maritime mayhem he highlights with his witty
pen and captures so admirably with his hilarious illustrations.

A great read for the armchair sailor – but you may decide that
the armchair is the safest place to stay!

The **Ups** and **Downs**
of a
Lockkeeper

Jake Kavanagh

ADLARD COLES NAUTICAL

B L O O M S B U R Y

LONDON • NEW DELHI • NEW YORK • SYDNEY

Published 2009 by Adlard Coles Nautical
an imprint of Bloomsbury Publishing Plc
50 Bedford Square, London WC1B 3DP
www.adlardcoles.com

First edition published 1991
Reprinted 1992, 1993, 1995, 1998
Reissued 2002
Reprinted 2006
Reissued 2009
Reprinted 2013

ISBN 978-1-4081-1441-4

A CIP catalogue record for this book is available
from the British Library.

This book is produced using paper that is made from wood grown
in managed, sustainable forests. It is natural, renewable and recyclable.
The logging and manufacturing processes conform to the
environmental regulations of the country of origin.

Printed and bound by CPI Group (UK) Ltd, Croydon, CR0 4YY

Note: while all reasonable care has been taken in the publication
of this book, the publisher takes no responsibility for the
use of the methods or products described in the book.

Contents

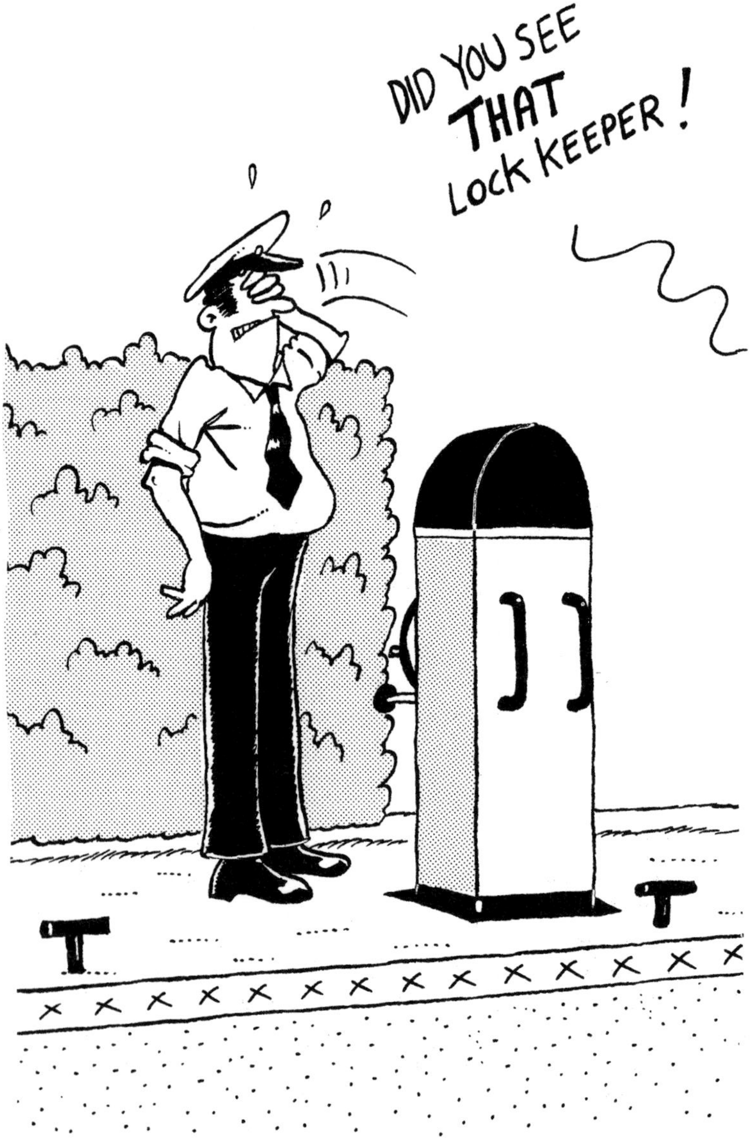
DID YOU SEE THAT LOCK KEEPER!

Introduction

Passer-by: 'Excuse me, but do you need a degree in hydrology to be a lockkeeper?'
Keeper: 'No sir. Just a sense of humour!'

Anyone who has ever enjoyed messing around in boats may well have had to use a lock at some time. Locks come in all shapes and sizes, from tiny brick-lined affairs on narrow-beamed canals, to state of the art concrete jobs at bustling high tech marinas. But they all have one thing in common. If they can catch you out, they will.

It isn't just the novices who come unstuck either. Marine mishaps can plague the best of us, and a lock, with its lack of room and milling fleet of potential targets, does tend to shorten the odds.

The hordes of sightseers who come to watch the antics of boaters give no applause for skilful pilotage. You can guide the boat into the chamber as though she were mounted on rails, dock her without even squeezing the fenders, and lasso a distant bollard with a casual flick of the wrist, and they will be totally unimpressed. But somersault off the fordeck in your designer yachtwear and plummet into the murky water below, and they will positively love you.

For several enjoyable years I worked as a relief keeper on the River Thames, moving between ten locks on one of the busiest sections of this scenic waterway. Almost inevitably, at the end of the season there were countless stories to be told by the keepers who had locked through nearly one million boats between them. This book is a collection of the best of these stories, most of them first hand and all of them true. It may seem like a catalogue of chaos to the uninitiated, but as regular boaters will know, when things are going well, using a lock is all part of the fun. But when things go wrong, there is always someone watching...

1

2

1

Lock us up

A lock assistant was hailed by a student on a narrowboat.'I'm afraid we've lost a pair of glasses overboard,' she said.'They're very expensive, so when you let the water out, can you drain the lock completely? Then we can walk along the bottom and have a look for them.'

What is a lock? In simple terms, a lock is a chamber enclosed between two sets of gates that allows boats to be floated from one level of water to another (see diagram on pages 102 and 103). In most cases locks will occur singly, but some canals in hilly country will have a whole string of them linked together to form a 'flight'. This prompted an innocent American to comment, 'Why have all these little locks? Why not put the whole thing on one level and have just one big lock in London?'

The majority of the locks on the waterway system are user-operated, including the manned ones 'after hours'. The most common mistake made by boaters working a lock themselves is to try to fill the chamber with the lower set of sluices still wide open (they are often left this way to keep the lock empty and so reduce the weed growth on the walls). As a result, the level in the chamber creeps slowly up to the half-way mark and eventually stays there, and after half an hour or so the boater will become a little concerned.

If the lock is manned, he will amble over to the lockkeeper's cottage and rap on the door. Murphy's Law says that the off-duty keeper will be either having his dinner or having a wash when he is disturbed, and may not always be the source of good humour when the boater solemnly tells him that his lock doesn't work. Equally solemnly, the lockkeeper will ask the boater if he has ever tried filling a bath with the plug out.

The hand winding mechanism causes occasional confusion

Some locks can be quite narrow and deep

Boaters' Spot Test Number One

Lock   Nomenclature

During the season, the various parts of a lock are referred to by many different names, some of which are listed below. Test your knowledge by ticking the ones that are correct (the answers are in the diagram at the back of the book).

You should secure your boat to...

☐   *a bollard*

☐   *a bullock*

☐   *a b*ll*ck*

☐   *that black mushroom thing*

☐   *whatever is in reach*

Water is admitted to the chamber by...

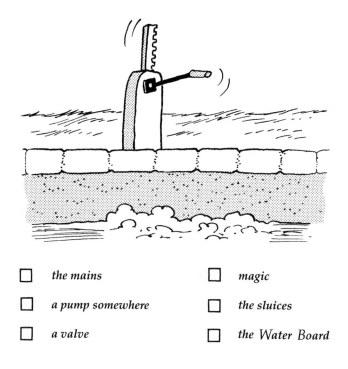

☐ the mains   ☐ magic

☐ a pump somewhere   ☐ the sluices

☐ a valve   ☐ the Water Board

You should address the man in charge as...

☐ Captain Birdseye/Haddock /
  Nemo/Bligh

☐ lockkeeper/master

☐ oy, you in the funny hat

☐ sailor

Sweating in the midday sun, a lockkeeper and his assistant were working hard to try to ease the queues that had grown each side of their lock. The assistant was having a difficult time with the owner of a flybridge cruiser who had stopped halfway down the chamber and was stubbornly refusing to move up.

'It gets too rough by the sluices,' he said, glaring down from his perch. 'You'll damage the hull.' The assistant was just about to make one last exasperated plea when he was tapped on the shoulder. 'Excuse me,' a rambler asked, 'but could you tell me why there are locks on this river?'

With a totally deadpan face, the assistant simply nodded towards the cruiser.

'To annoy the boaters, of course,' he replied.

One of the most enjoyable aspects of a lockkeeper's job is answering questions, many of which are about the basic operation of the lock itself, although sometimes indirectly. Take the smartly dressed businessman on a hospitality boat that had just moored up in the chamber. 'Hey, why have we stopped?' he asked. 'You're in a lock, sir,' the keeper replied as he walked towards the sluices.

'A what?'

The keeper explained what was going to happen: how he was going to let the water out so that the steamer would float down to the lower level. 'I see,' said the businessman. 'Very clever.' Then he began looking around with a frown on his face. 'So tell me, where is the one you use for going up?'

A narrowboat with a family of six aboard ran hard aground behind a weir one evening, so the lockkeeper rowed out to them to offer his assistance. As he probed the riverbed around the hull with a pole, he asked the skipper why he had taken his boat into such an awkward spot.

'Well, we were all pretty tired,' the skipper explained, 'and we didn't want to have to work the lock by ourselves. So we thought we'd find a way around it...'

There are several types of lock

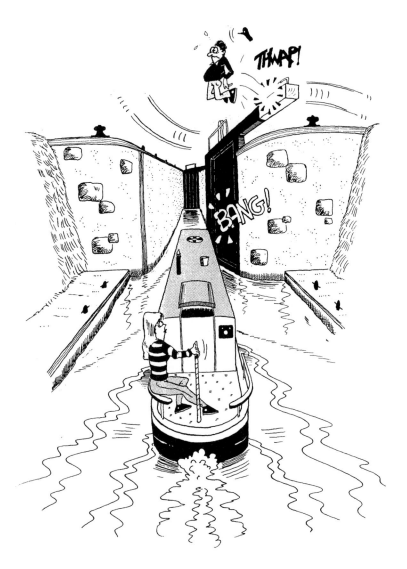

1. Manual balance beam gates

2. Guillotine gates

3. Electric roll gates

4. *Large capacity sea locks*

Weirs often encroach onto the main navigation channel

2

Weir'd happenings

Comment from a lady after passing the long sweeping overspill of Marlow weir: 'That's a really pretty waterfall you've got back there. Does it actually do anything, or is it just for show?'

On most navigable rivers, and some canals, the lockkeeper has to look after the nearby weir. A weir is simply an adjustable dam, and by raising or lowering a set of sluice gates incorporated into the structure, the keeper can control the level of water in the reach above his lock. It all involves a certain amount of guesswork, and during the boating season when a whole armada of cruisers could be moored with just a few inches of water beneath their keels, he doesn't have much of a margin for error.

Some weirs are remarkably basic affairs: little more than a submerged wall beside the river that is exposed when the water level drops too low, thus cutting off the flow. Others are far more complex arrangements of steel and concrete, with heavy-duty winches working sluice gates which can sometimes weigh several tons apiece. Part of the keeper's job is to ensure that these gates stay free of the inevitable flotsam that finds its way into the river - items such as old beer barrels, traffic cones, tree trunks and, alas, the occasional motor cruiser.

A hireboat cast off from its yard and headed merrily downriver. A few minutes later the yard received a call that it was stranded on a weir, and their beefy little tug was quickly dispatched to help. A line was passed aboard, and the boat, pinned broadside against the whitewashed safety piles but otherwise undamaged, was snatched away from danger.

'Why did you go onto the weir?' the shaken hirer was asked. 'Didn't you see the signpost marked 'Channel'?'

The hirer nodded. 'Oh yes,' he said, 'But I didn't want to go down the Channel, did I. I wanted to go down the Thames!'

'Look, Dad. He's found a short cut!'

Bridge heights are all measured from zero on the 'head water' gauge

The water held above a weir is known as 'head' water, and you will usually be able to spot a measuring gauge somewhere near the bullnose of the lock. The ideal level of the river is at zero on the gauge, and as all the bridge heights are measured from this zero mark, the keeper has to adjust his weir in such a way that the level doesn't stray too far above or below it. And the water isn't always obliging. So if you hear the owner of a tall motor cruiser ask the lockkeeper, 'How's the head today?', he isn't enquiring after the lockkeeper's hangover. He wants to know the exact height of the water level, because just a few inches difference could amputate his radome at the next low bridge.

A large sea-going motoryacht had penetrated some thirty miles upstream from the estuary when it was stopped by a notoriously low footbridge over a lock-cut. As the boat was marginally too tall to pass under it, the lockkeeper opened his weir and dropped the water level as much as he dared. Unfortunately it wasn't enough, so the owner partially flooded his bilges and asked a few passers-by to step aboard to weigh the boat down even further. Despite all these efforts, they still needed two more inches to clear the bridge.

'I give up!' said the exasperated owner. 'I'll have to turn back.'

'Well, there is one last thing we haven't tried,' said the keeper. 'May I take the controls?'

He backed the boat off until she was a short distance from the bridge, straightened her up and then, to the owner's horror, rammed both throttles to full ahead. The huge diesels bellowed, the propellors dug deep, and as the boat lunged forward she sat down heavily at the stern - so heavily, in fact, that the bridge skimmed harmlessly overhead with an inch to spare. As soon as they were clear, the keeper throttled back to neutral and grinned at the poor man's ashen face.

'Show a lady who's boss,' he said as he patted the wheel, 'and she'll bob you a little curtsey...'

Late one night an angler knocked on the lockkeeper's door and breathlessly told him that a boat was wrecked on his weir and that there were still survivors on board. The weir at Romney is a large modern affair stretching between the wooded banks of the weir stream, and when the rescuers had run along the catwalk and switched on the floodlights, they couldn't believe their eyes. Jammed at a crazy angle beneath them was a tiny cabin cruiser, and in the cockpit were six incredibly drunk young 'survivors'.

They were also incredibly lucky. The boat had hit the lip of a partially submerged gate at such speed that she had carried on right over it, and only a horizontal supporting strut just beyond had caught the bow and prevented a nosedive into the swirling weir pool below.

The survivors simply didn't appreciate the precariousness of their perch, and were in the middle of a noisy argument when the rescuers arrived. Once ashore, and slightly sobered up, the owner explained what had happened.

They had been moored outside a riverside pub, and after an enormous binge they had decanted themselves into their boat and roared off into the night. 'I gave the helm to my girlfriend,' he said, 'and told her to just follow the river. I bent down to open some beers, and next thing I know, she's put us on the weir!' He scowled in the poor girl's direction. 'Women drivers!' he muttered.

Weirs are enjoyed by fishermen and canoeists alike

Lockkeepers are very proud of their ability to finely tune their weirs, and one keeper was dismayed to see the water level dropping sharply when it should have been steadily rising. He jumped on his bicycle and pedalled up to his weir to investigate. The problem soon became apparent. A canoeist, resplendent in yellow waterproofs and life-jacket, was cheerfully pulling a whole set of small radial gates out of the weir.

'What the hell do you think you're doing?' the keeper yelled above the roar of escaping water.

'Don't worry,' chirped the canoeist. 'I'm just making it a bit rougher for my canoe!'

3

Spring is sprung

An entry in the incident book of a rural lock on the Thames reads: '6.55am Sunday. Telephone enquiry from a gentleman wishing to know if the current was too strong for his four-horsepower outboard engine. Advised the gent where to stick his four-horsepower outboard engine at this hour on a Sunday morning.'

Spring is a busy time for the lock staff. As winter releases her icy grip and the days slowly draw out again, so the preparations begin to get everything ready for the busy season ahead.

Apart from being beautiful, spring can also be frustrating. The first rays of sunshine that are opening blossoms everywhere are also opening the covers of winterised boats, and an assortment of pre-season boaters begins arriving at the gates with appalling irregularity. The lawnmower that has only decided to start after fifty pulls, half a can of rocket fuel and some fairly imaginitive swear words has to be stopped again on the arrival of a small boat 'just out for a spin'.

As soon as the keeper goes to let the cruiser through, the mower returns to hibernation. So 20 minutes later the keeper finds himself tugging on the starter cord and loudly cursing the father of the internal combustion engine before stomping away to find a tool kit. After a service that verges on a rebore, the mower reluctantly bursts into life again, and with a sigh of relief the keeper wipes his hands, packs away his tools and then wheels the spluttering machine to the offending patch of grass. He is just about to throw it into gear when a figure that is vaguely familiar appears beside him.

'Hullo!' chirps the boater. 'Can you let me back down again?'

The locks also consume paint in huge quantities. The bulk of the work can usually be done in the winter, but a certain amount of touching up is required before the season starts in earnest. Unfortunately, the paint the makers claim can withstand 'storms, hail, frost and extreme variations in temperature' is helpless against cruisers, and a liberal coating on the mooring piles and lay-by will be lucky to make it to the end of the season.

As a result, early spring can become something of a contest between the boaters, who are perfectly entitled to use the locks, and the lock staff, who are desperately trying to paint them.

'Wet paint? I didn't see any...'

'I'm sure they said this lock was manned.'

Whilst spring cruising can involve deserted rivers, silent marinas, and mist-shrouded canals, it can also mean torrential rain. If this persists over a number of days the rivers begin to rise, and the lockkeepers begin pulling more and more gates out of the weirs to compensate. After a while the current may be so strong that it is said to be 'enhanced', and the hireboats (which are not insured for such dangerous conditions) are stopped from cruising unless they have a qualified pilot aboard.

It is not a pleasant task for a lockkeeper to have to tell a hirer to stop his holiday and hand the controls over to a complete stranger. It is even less pleasant when the hirer disbelieves him...

Several days of torrential rain had swelled the river to twice its normal size, and a hireboat was having a tremendous battle to make any headway. Pushing a bow wave like an attacking destroyer, she gained yard after tortuous yard from the swirling grey water until she finally clawed her way into the tranquillity of the lock-cut. Having moored in the lock, the skipper, a large and stern-looking man, was handed a warning notice from the lockkeeper. The notice explained the danger and asked him to ring his boatyard and request a pilot.

'What utter rubbish!' the man said. 'There's nothing wrong with this river at all. This is just a clever security ploy.'

The keeper looked at him with baffled amazement, until he remembered that the Queen was due to open the new regatta building in Henley the following day. Security was bound to be tight, but how on earth do you lay on a flood? He tried to point out the nearby weir with its thundering water and clouds of leaping spray, but the boater was convinced it was all an elaborate trick. 'You can't fool me,' he snapped. 'I'm a police officer. If the hireboat people are going to behave like this, they can have their bloody boat back.'

The keeper shrugged and guided the boater to a phone from where he could heap his wrath upon the unfortunate hirefleet operator.

'I've been accused of many thing over the years,' the keeper said later, 'but that was the first time I've deliberately flooded the river for security reasons!'

...there is always one.

Rainfall, sir? Aye, we've had a drop or two...

Sometimes, after prolonged rainfall or the thaw of winter snow, a river can rise above the ability of the weirs to contain it. Every single gate is pulled out, but it is simply not enough. Nature finally overwhelms man's impressive efforts to control her. The owners of expensive riverside properties watch in growing apprehension as the last garden gnome disappears under water, the goldfish pond becomes tidal, and the river continues to inch relentlessly towards the living room...

Rising levels can make quite a difference in the operation of a lock, and a problem that often affects boaters is the flooding of the lockside. It is quite common for the head level to spill over the locksides when the chamber has filled. This happened to the owner of a small cruiser who was making his way upriver after several days of rain. He was standing beside the bollards and holding his ropes when the water crept over the edge and insidiously began to fill his shoes.

'Lockkeeper! For heaven's sake, stop!' he cried, as he hopped and splashed beside his boat. 'You're letting too much water in.'

4

A helping hand

Boater: 'Where can I tie my boat up, please?'
Assistant (pointing): 'Those are the piles you moor on.'
Boater: 'How dare you call me a moron!'

Almost anyone can be an assistant lockkeeper. There are no formal qualifications for the job - all that is asked of applicants is that they should be physically fit and able to swim. As with most summer jobs, the ideal employees are students, but the start of the boating season is far too early for them, so the employers have to look elsewhere. The busy coastal marinas often take people on to help out at weekends, or just during the height of the season, whilst British Waterways, with the bulk of their 1500 locks worked by boaters, only need temporary staff for special research projects. On the Thames, however, there is a constant demand for assistants in the summer, and employment can last from April to as late as October, depending on the location.

A few years ago, a keeper was sent a rather odd young man. He looked like a failed hippy, with a thin nervous body, straggly black hair and wide staring eyes, but he soon got the hang of the lock, so the keeper was able to get on with his garden without keeping a constant eye on the lockside. The peace was soon shattered, however, when a small boy pointed out a dead fish floating belly-up in the chamber.

With a monumental splash, the assistant hurled himself into the water and began to swim purposefully towards the bobbing fish. Drawing close, he scooped its bloated body into his hands and swam to the stairwell, still holding the fish as he climbed the steps. Finally - to the horror of the astonished boaters - he sat down on a bollard, lifted the fish's head to his lips and began to administer artificial respiration with almost textbook precision.

Summoned by the commotion, the lockkeeper dropped his spade and came hurrying out of his garden. Somewhat puzzled, he approached the dripping young man, who was hunched over the fish blowing slowly and deliberately into its disintegrating mouth.

'What the hell do you think you're doing?' he asked, echoing the thoughts of the gathering crowd of onlookers.

The assistant's head jerked up. 'I've got to save this fish!' he snapped. He fixed the keeper with an unnerving stare before turning back to the long-dead perch.

The lockkeeper, however, recovered quickly. 'Well, would you mind telling me why?'

The assistant looked up again, and spat out a few loose scales. 'Because,' he said, pointing a trembling finger to the heavens, 'I've just had a vision from God.'

Divine intervention wasn't mentioned in the contract, but they sacked him anyway.

A knowledgeable assistant at a small Thames lock found himself answering questions from two young men on a hire boat. 'Is there any way we can get to the Norfolk Broads from here?' he was asked.

'Yes, there is,' the assistant replied cautiously, 'but you'll have to go downriver through twelve locks, work the tide through central London, negotiate the Barrier, then go out of the estuary, round the East Coast and go in again at Great Yarmouth.'

The skipper looked disheartened. 'Well that's no good,' he said. 'We've got to be back by six.'

Despite the requirement that all assistants be able to swim, not all are particularly buoyant. One poor fellow was catapulted into the water by a misplaced rope, and to everyone's surprise he began to scream and splash around in the water as though his time had come. He was thrown a lifering and ignominiously dragged to the stairwell.

'I thought you said you could swim,' the keeper growled.

'I can,' replied the assistant, 'but not in water that deep.'

One assistant at a busy lock had the annoying habit of leaping into the cockpits of people's boats if he felt they weren't handling them too well. Not that he was any better than they were, he just enjoyed the heroics. One day, however, he did it just once too often. Having jumped aboard a large hireboat, he suddenly let out a yell and jumped out again, a look of sheer terror on his face. Under the circumstances, this was quite understandable: just inches from his behind were the snapping teeth of a very large dog indeed...

During a particularly hot summer, an assistant keeper developed a stunt at the end of the day which hardly ever failed. He would ask a hireboat crew to throw him their stern rope and then, apparently struggling with the line, he would cry 'Whoa skipper, careful!' before tumbling dramatically into the water. The crew were invariably appalled, and although they could never quite work out how they had caused the accident, they were always very apologetic and plied their victim with beer. Which only served to encourage him.

A lockkeeper couldn't explain why his assistant became dreamy and distant after smoking a roll-up cigarette...

...until he discovered a new variety of pot plants thriving in his greenhouse.

Mowing the lawns is a regular part of the assistant's job. When it comes to the steeply angled banks often found outside the chamber there is a special technique. A petrol-driven hover mower is swung across the bank on the end of a length of rope, rather like a giant pendulum, and is controlled by the operator from the safety of the path above.

When an over-enthusiastic assistant lost his footing and let go of the rope, he could only watch in horror as the mower slid down the bank towards the river, gathering speed all the way. At the bottom of the bank, and almost level with the water, it hit a concrete landing stage with a loud metallic clang. Speed unchecked, the perfectly balanced machine skimmed out across the water like a small ugly hovercraft. It had travelled an impressive distance on its air cushion before it clipped one of the mooring posts and flipped over, plunging beneath the surface in an explosion of spray and blue exhaust smoke. It took several minutes, and the appearance of a small oil slick, for the bewildered assistant to convince the keeper what had happened.

A certain steamer skipper used to enjoy playing practical jokes on boaters and passengers alike. His favourite was to steer his 100 ton vessel through crowded waters whilst wearing dark glasses and clutching a white stick.

5

The Professionals

A guide on a tripper boat was pointing out some historical landmarks to a group of American tourists as they cruised towards Staines.

'And on our right,' she said, 'is the field of Runnymede, where King John signed the famous Magna Carta in 1215.'

'Hell, we've missed it,' drawled one of the party. 'Its one o'clock already.'

On most of the popular waterways you are bound to see tripper boats. They are a curious collection, many originally powered by steam engine, which has left them the general term of 'steamer'. Most have been converted to diesel, some have been specially built, others have been refitted over the years, but all are carefully inspected by the Department of Transport at the start of each season. The skippers are all DoT qualified, and many have been plying their particular patch of waterway for years. Hardened professionals, you might say, and you'd be right. So there can't be any problems with steamers, surely...?

Fog can be a nuisance in the early part of the season, and some real pea-soupers can reduce visibility almost to nil. During one of these, a steamer was carefully following the shadowy outline of the bank when her sister ship loomed out of the fog ahead. They altered course smartly to avoid a head on collision, and as they drifted past each other, one skipper shouted to the other, 'Where are you going?'

'Windsor,' came the confident reply.

The questioner frowned. 'You can't be!' he called back, 'that's where I'm going!'

Passenger steamers on the Thames are not allowed to have priority at a busy lock, although the keeper will usually alter the order of entry so that these large and unwieldy vessels are the first in their batch to enter (if they lose reverse, they only thing they can hit is the gates). Some steamer skippers, however, will occasionally try to queue-jump if they are running late, and heated discussions with pleasure boaters can follow.

When a new summer assistant appeared at the controls of a notorious bottle-neck lock during a hectic bank holiday, the skipper of a waiting steamer took advantage of his naivity. He made his way to the foredeck, picked his moment, and then hailed the assistant. As the young man looked down at him, the skipper held up his thumb and asked, 'Are you OK, mate?' The assistant was pleased by this comradely enquiry about his health, and returned the thumbs up sign with a cheery 'Yeah, OK mate!'

The skipper immediately shouted to his crew, 'Lockkeeper has called us in!' Even as the stunned assistant was lowering the offending thumb, the steamer was slipping her lines and making for the empty chamber. The thirty or so cruiser owners who had missed a lock were a bit upset about that.

Lockkeepers usually prefer to put large vessels at the front of a lock

Steamer skippers all have to pass a searching examination before being let loose with any form of commercial passenger boat. The core of professional full-time staff is topped up by the recruitment of casual deckhands in the season, and now and again someone is taken on when perhaps it would have been better to have left them ashore.

When the skipper of a steamer on a regular tripping run found himself caught short, he handed the wheel to the nearest crewman before diving below. The reach was wide and comparatively empty, so he felt he had time on his hands to answer the scream of nature. But as the steamer rounded a bend in the river she found herself right in the middle of a major sailing regatta. The crewman didn't have a clue as to what action to take.

Normally, a motor vessel should throttle back and pull over to the right-hand side of the river, aiming to pass astern of the tacking boats. This crewman, however, maintained his speed and course and opened a path through the forest of sails like the Red Sea before Moses.

The race dissolved into total chaos as 90 feet of fast moving steel made a totally unexpected appearance in its midst, and the cries of horror and outrage were accompanied by the flapping of sails and the clanging of spars.

Just as the crewman thought he had emerged without hitting anyone, a straggler cut across his bows. There was a crunch, a shout, and then the dinghy's mast smacked down on the water. As the upturned wreck swept past the wheelhouse, the crewman finally throttled back and looked around for survivors, but to his dismay there was no-one in sight.

'What the hell happened?' cried the horrified skipper, appearing beside him in the wheelhouse. The crewman was about to reply when an elderly lady addressed them from the foredeck.

'Excuse me,' she said, 'but there's a man hanging from the railing!'

Incredible as it may seem, the dinghy sailor had leapt up at the steamer just as it ran down his boat, and was hanging grimly from the lower rail like a long yellow fender. The astonished crew rushed forward and pulled him aboard, and were treated to a full broadside of abuse for their trouble.

The case was duly reported to both the Water Authority and the steamer company, who were suitably appalled. The skipper and crewman were ordered to fill out separate accident report forms, but the crewman found that he needed some help.

'What do I put under 'cause of accident'?' he asked.

'Don't make anything up,' he was warned. 'In your own words, just tell the truth.' Well, the truth is what they got.

'I knocked the boat over,' he wrote, 'because I was so drunk I couldn't see nothing.'

And to his surprise, they fired him.

6

The Boaters

A lockkeeper was hailed by the owner of a large and particularly noisy motor cruiser: 'Where do you want me to go, lockkeeper?'
Keeper (wearily): 'How about the Atlantic, sir?'

As most long-suffering boaters will realise, come the sunny summer weekends at the more popular venues, you can spend more time queueing for the locks than actually cruising on the waters they serve. Clearing these queues as quickly and as good-humouredly as possible depends as much on the skill of the boater as on that of the lockkeeper.

A summer assistant was once incensed by a small boy who wandered up to the lockside from a waiting cruiser. 'Daddy says you're not working the lock very well,' he announced, which immediately endeared him to the hard-working lock staff.

'Oh does he?' growled the assistant.

'Oh, yes,' replied the boy. 'You see, in the last lock, you only had four boats. But in the lock before that you had seven. Daddy says that if you got seven boats in every lock then we wouldn't have to queue.'

The assistant gave him a withering look. 'You tell your daddy,' he said at last, 'that if all the boats were the same bloomin' size, then we bloomin' well would!'

Apart from the small percentage of professional boatmen, the remainder of lock traffic consists of leisure boaters. Although the privately-owned boats far outnumber those in the hire-fleets, it is the latter that put in most of the mileage. Thus the hireboater becomes the lockkeeper's most frequent customer, especially during the week.

Throughout the canal network and along the more popular navigable rivers there are a number of boatyards offering comfortable cruisers for hire. 'No experience necessary,' some of the brochures proclaim. 'Handling a boat is simpler than driving a car!'...which can be a bit misleading. The controls are simpler, most certainly, but how many cars have you seen drifting sideways whilst stationary? Consequently, the occasional hirer does rather expect his 60ft steel narrowboat weighing 14 tons to be just as manoeuvrable as his five-speed hatchback - which can lead to some interesting situations in a crowded lock.

One poor fellow had got himself into a terrible pickle. He had crashed into virtually everything in sight, and was on the verge of giving up his holiday in disgust when the lockkeeper came to his rescue.

'Is there anyone in your crew who doesn't drive a car?' he asked.

'My daughter,' came the reply, 'She's not old enough yet.'

'Well, put her on the wheel and see how you get on.'

In desperation, the boater agreed, and was instantly amazed. The 14-year-old girl handled the boat beautifully, mainly because she allowed for the fact that it was very much afloat, and not anchored to a road by two pairs of steel-braced radials.

It is this transition from motorcar to motorboat that causes most of the problems, and for a total novice it can take a little getting used to. The hire-fleet operators make a valiant effort to give their customers some training (it increases their chances of getting the boat back in one piece) but at the height of the season, when the whole fleet could need refuelling and cleaning at the same time, there is often only time for the basics.

Most first-time hirers find driving up the river easy enough, but when they are faced with a steep-sided lock chamber and a boat that is suddenly unresponsive to the helm, a mild case of panic can set in. The keeper is often there to take their ropes, and offer some advice if he's asked. But not everyone who hires a boat is new to the game, not by a long way.

A suntanned teenager on the stern of a hirecraft was in the process of unravelling his tangled rope when the over-helpful lockkeeper reached out from the lockside and took it from his hands. 'I'll sort that out for you, sonny,' he said cheerfully. 'Here, I'll show you how to tie a bowline as well. Find the end, like this. then make a small loop, okay? Bunny comes out of the hole, goes round the tree...'

The young man watched patiently without saying a word, and finally took the rope back once the keeper had completed the knot. 'Get the idea?' the keeper asked. The young man said yes, he could probably manage it. As the keeper walked past the cockpit to get to the pedestal, a woman at the helm beckoned him over.

'You shouldn't really have done that,' she whispered. 'You see, he's in the British Olympic sailing team.'

The record for the maximum number of collisions in the shortest stretch of river is held by three burly men in a 28ft Elysian. They always seemed to overrun their stopping distance, and shunted gates, cruisers and bullnoses with alarming regularity. After one quite spectacular crunch, the skipper sheepishly admitted to a keeper that he found the boat chronically underpowered, especially after helming a boat of his own for more than 20 years.

'Oh, what sort of boat have you got?' asked the keeper.

'A steel job,' said the man. 'A 2000-ton tug on the Humber.'

Car withdrawal syndrome doesn't just extend to the manoeuvring of a boat - it covers the mechanics as well. The most common form of propulsion amongst hire cruisers is the diesel engine, which is usually started by a key and button, and stopped by pulling on a decompressor lever. Most of the engine breakdowns in a lock are simply a result of the boater forgetting to re-engage the decompression lever once its been used. One young lady had almost flattened the battery with the starter motor before she noticed the offending lever standing proud of the dashboard.

'No wonder it wouldn't go,' she exclaimed, slapping it home. 'I left the handbrake on.'

The lockkeeper is always ready to catch your ropes

When a boater was overheard complaining about his engine running hot, a passer-by ventured a solution.

'It's probably your weed filter,' he said. 'Take it out and give it a good blow.' He was referring to the filter, of course, but the boater thought he meant the boat. So, following the advice, he took it out and gave it a good blow - full throttle up and down the reach until the poor engine boiled over and siezed! A little knowledge is a dangerous thing.

The rather erratic high-speed approach of a small cruiser put the keeper of a small rural lock on his guard. As the boat swept in through the gates, the keeper realised that she was rapidly running out of stopping distance, so he shouted a timely warning. 'OK, skipper, go astern now!'

'Righty ho!' said the skipper, and to the lockkeeper's horror, he promptly abandoned the controls and made his way to the back of the boat!

Speeders are a pest on the waterways

Weekends on the river will see a surge of privately-owned cruisers, and most of their owners are a good-natured bunch of enthusiasts. They enjoy being afloat, and they take a great pride in their craft, which is why they are terrified of being shunted in a lock - or anywhere else for that matter. One drawback with actually owning a boat, however, is that you are automatically deemed to be an expert, whether you are or not.

Hire-craft can bounce off as many lock gates, lay-bys or police launches as they like, and usually be forgiven as being novices. But the larger and more sparkling a privately-owned boat, the better the skipper is expected to be at handling her; and as everyone knows, a lock is not the best of places to find out.

A motorcruiser was heading towards a collision when a boater yelled across the water.

'Look out! Go full ahead astern!'

It is tempting to think that because people are at the controls of their own boat, they will be au fait with all the nautical terminology. A lot are, but an equal number are not. As some of the hirers will still be suffering from car withdrawal symptoms, it is best not to blind them with a barrage of salty sayings. Forget bow and stern, it's 'front' and 'back'. Warps end up as 'rope' - or 'string' if you're desperate - and fenders should be referred to as 'round things' or 'balloons'. As many of the lock staff are ex-Navy men, de-nauticalising themselves can often be the hardest part of the job...

Most boat owners are a good-natured bunch of enthusiasts

A keeper was chatting with the owner of a seagoing motorboat in his lock when he noticed that the aft line had come adrift.

'Look out,' he said. 'Your stern's swinging.'

The owner sat up and looked anxiously around the decks.

'Stern?' he asked. 'What's that?'

The keeper pointed frantically at the back of the boat.

'Oh!' said the owner, leaping to his feet, 'you mean the arse end.'

You can always spot the experts because...

The skipper is calm and in total control

The deckhands are familiar with simple knots such as the bowline

The crew are all alert and poised for action

On approaching a lock, the fenders are down and correctly positioned

A well-dressed lady on an immaculate 35-footer was anxious that her husband was approaching the lock too fast whilst the fenders were still on deck.

'Jeremy!' she cried, in a voice that carried to everyone, 'we're going to bang. Quick, dangle your balls over the side!'

When dealing with boaters generally, the lockkeeper needs to be a diplomat. Apart from anything else, he has no way of knowing the relationship between the people on board (although it is often fun to guess!). As a result, such terms as 'wife', 'husband' or (especially) 'daughter' should be avoided. The trick is to address them with the general terms of 'skipper' and 'crew'. This can often lead to hilarity ('if he's the skipper, then I'm the fairy godmother', and so on) but it is far safer than inadvertently referring to some executive's girlfriend as his grand-daughter, or worse!

Never assume that the crew of a boat are married

'I soon put the lockkeeper in his place, dear '

Most of the locks on the Thames keep a selection of postcards for the public to buy, and one keeper was updating his display when a small cruiser nosed her way into the chamber, her skipper singlehanding her downstream. The keeper nodded a greeting, and then jabbed a thumb at the postcard rack.

'Got one here with your boat on it,' he grinned.

The man at the helm was obviously pleased. 'Really?'

'Oh yes. You and your wife upstream somewhere.' He plucked the card from the rack and handed it to the skipper, whose face fell instantly.

'Oh my gawd!'

'What's up?' asked the keeper, 'don't you like it?'

'Like it?' The man turned the card around and pointed to the scantily-clad woman pictured on the foredeck. 'Lockkeeper,' he said, in a voice choked with panic, 'that's not my wife!'

Boaters Spot Test Number Two

Hand Signals

Pictured below is a uniformed lockkeeper. Tick the box which contains the correct interpretation of each hand signal.

- ☐ *Stop!*
- ☐ *Greetings*
- ☐ *I want five boats*

- ☐ *That side please*
- ☐ *I am exercising my finger*
- ☐ *Look, there is a quack quack*

☐ Come ahead

☐ Stay tied up and ignore me as I am deliberately waving you into a collision

☐ Hello, I am a friendly lockkeeper. Please wave back.

☐ I have a hangover

☐ Enter the lock with your eyes shut

☐ I didn't see that shunt, so I don't have to do the paperwork

☐ Is the kettle on?

☐ May I borrow your boom - I wish to hang myself

☐ There is no way you'll clear the next low bridge

Should you tip a lockkeeper?

If you have ever cruised through the French canals, you will know that a small gift of a can of beer or a packet of cigarettes to an Eclusier will have your good name buzzing down the telephone lines to his colleagues (if you haven't got any ciggies, and are teetotal, buy some of his home-grown vegetables instead. It's just as effective).

In the United Kingdom, some manned waterways encourage a small gratuity to a lockkeeper who has just ruptured himself working you through with pre-war machinery, but the busy River Thames is strictly a no-tipping navigation. An exchange of cash could be construed as bribery, and having been hit between the eyes by a pound coin thrown at extreme range, I imagine there could be a safety aspect involved as well. But don't worry. On a warm day, a can of beer will be gratefully received by the hard-working lock staff.

When a tired old narrowboat broke down in a lock near Maidenhead the relief lockkeeper went out of his way to help. A keen mechanic he soon effected repairs, and was delighted to learn that the grateful skipper was nothing less than a sales representative for a well-known brewery. The keeper was handed a whole case of 'sample' beer for his trouble, and carried his prize back to the lock intending to have a monumental booze-up. But his hopes were dashed on closer examination of the cans. It was a completely new brand, and all of it was alcohol-free!

On a warm day...

...a can of beer is a welcome treat

'That's why I'll never buy a fibreglass boat '

7

Things that go bump
in a lock

A cruiser was weaving all over the lock-cut when her skipper hailed the keeper.
'Which side of the lock do you want me to go, lockkeeper?'
'Inside would be nice, sir...'

Whilst a lock can have all sorts of surprises in store for the unwary boater, there are a number of mishaps that occur with such alarming regularity that they have even been given names by the lock staff. Here are some of the most popular ways of denting the boat (and ego) whilst locking through.

The Doodlebug

Perhaps the most horrendous manoeuvre a boat can make in a lock is the doodlebug. This can often involve a particularly large and heavy steel narrowboat and a lock that is jammed with expensive GRP cruisers. The root cause of the problem is that car-to-boat transition again. In a car, you can't use reverse while still moving forwards, so some people assume that it must be the same for a boat. As a result, a skipper (and not always a novice, by the way) will line up his 14-ton vessel with a lock, give a final burst of forward gear, and then calmly turn the engine off.

As with the World War II flying bomb which gave this manoeuvre its name, there is a heart-stopping silence as the steel projectile hurtles towards its target, and the keeper has just a few seconds in which to act. If he's lucky, the boater will throw him a rope, and thus give him the chance to apply the Handbrake. This is a rolling turn around a bollard, slowly paid out to bring the boat to a halt. A successful Handbrake, however, does depend on two factors. Firstly, that the rope is actually tied to the boat (it is embarrassing when the boater's hastily-tied knot comes adrift just as the pressure is taken up, and the keeper describes a dainty backward flip into his flowerbed). And secondly, that the Doodlebug is on a manned side of the lock. If it's on the other side, all the keeper can do is scream, 'Start the engine and shove it in reverse quick as you bloody well can!', by which time the boat has probably buried her nose in another man's dream.

Two incorrect remedies to the Doodlebug are the John Wayne and the Bow-thruster. The John Wayne involves a boater leaping ashore with a rope and being towed down the lockside by his runaway vessel. When a lockkeeper pointed to a bollard and shouted, 'Take a turn,' one boater replied, 'Righty-ho,' spun on his heel, and got towed along backwards.

The John Wayne

The Bow-thruster

With the Bow-thruster, rather than checking a boat using the stern rope, a crewman will stop her with the bow rope. If he puts a locking turn onto a bollard, the effects are quite spectacular. The nose of the vessel is snatched against the wall with a deafening crash, whilst the stern swings across the lock and invariably crunches into another boat. One canalboat struck the wall so hard that a large window fell out of its mountings and vanished into the chamber. The hirer's deposit did a similar vanishing trick when he took the boat back to its yard.

The Torpedo

Unlike the Doodlebug, the engine keeps going in a Torpedo, even after impact. The usual cause is failure of the gearbox or throttle cable at the most crucial moment, so the engine stays locked in gear.

A famous torpedo involved a small cruiser coming into a lock quite skilfully, until she engaged reverse gear. The cable parted, and the boat began to surge backwards out of the lock again, colliding with two cruisers that were innocently following her in. The steering took the opportune moment to jam hard to starboard, and the boat - now totally out of control - ended up describing tight backward circles in the weir pool until the stunned owners could work out what to do.

'Not now, son. The timing of this is critical...'

The Domino

Another variation of the Doodlebug, the Domino needs at least two cruisers to be moored in a lock with fairly loose lines. A third cruiser approaches, kills the engine, avoids all attempts at Handbrakes and John Waynes, and carries so much momentum that she shunts the first cruiser heavily up the transom. She in turn runs forwards and shunts the second, and so on. Fun to watch, but murder on the paintwork.

The Domino

The Hang-up

'Is that why they call them higher craft?'

Hang-ups occur when the water level in a lock drops away and leaves the boat behind. The most common cause of this is the gunwale of a boat catching on the lockside, or one of the ropes being left tied while the crewman goes to look at the postcards. With a horrible graunch, the boat starts to tip over, and the lockkeeper has to close the sluices quickly and flood the chamber again before any damage is done. Occasionally, he can be just a little too late, and with a violent bang the rope will part and the boat will crash back into the water, sometimes throwing her crew overboard in the process.

Never cut a rope that is taut, by the way. Stand well clear to avoid whiplash, grab hold of something to keep your balance, and pray the cleat is well secured to the deck.

The Pin-down

This happens less often than the Hang-up, and is caused by a boat being allowed to run too far forward as the water level rises. The nose will get itself jammed under one of the horizontal beams that reinforce the gate, and the next thing that happens is that the propeller and half the hull pop up for inspection. Happily, most Pin-downs have been extracted without serious damage once the lock has been reversed.

The Pincer

The Pincer involves closing the gates on a boat that hasn't quite passed through them. It is easily done, because the controls or balance beams on the tail set of gates are often some way from the lockside, so the operator's vision is partially obscured. Quite an alarming Pincer movement happened to a group of Germans on a narrowboat on the canals. They had moored too close to the back of the lock, and when the gates were shut, the long steel rudder was sandwiched between them. For some reason, the crew hadn't noticed, and as the lock began to fill, the increased pressure on the gates clamped the rudder in a vice-like grip. After a few moments, the Germans were horrified to see the water rising up the hull whilst the boat stayed exactly where she was. By the time they had reversed the lock, it was too late. The water surged aboard, and once the rudder was released again, the boat quietly sank, fortunately without danger to the crew.

The Hitch

Boathooks are an absolute menace. It is a common sight to see a crewman perched on the foredeck and wielding a boathook like a battle-crazed Sir Lancelot. He will jab at anything and everything that goes past, and invariably the tip will either slide on the smooth lock walls or jam in an unforeseen obstruction. One lockkeeper was very nearly deprived of his manhood when a lady slipped whilst fending off. Ever since then, he has seriously considered wearing a box.

Some other mishaps you may have seen (or done!)

The Snooker

The Deluge

The Suspender

The Sandwich

The Limbo

The Moby Dick

The Swan Lake

8

Falling in

A question from a drunken member of a rowdy booze-cruise:
'Had any showers here today, lockkeeper?'
'Only you lot, sir.'

Falling in is one of the most popular mishaps, and with so many people going for unscheduled swims in the locks, the antics of the boaters have become something of a spectator sport amongst the general public.

The lockkeeper's term for someone who falls in is SPLASHER, which stands for a Surprised Person Leaving A Ship Hurredly and Entering River. I have done it twice in full uniform, and on both occasions earned a round of applause and a large Scotch for my trouble. Since then, I have had profound sympathy for anyone who tumbles overboard in front of an audience, however much their performance is appreciated.

A boater had kept his boat at the same pontoon for many years, and always moored her port side to. One day, the boatyard moved him to a different berth, and moored him starboard side to instead. That night, the owner visited the boat to check some work on her. When he came to leave, he was so immersed in thought that he forgot about the recent move, and stepped off the boat to port as usual...

It was an awesome collision that jettisoned the crewman from the stern of his boat one weekend. The throttle linkage on his Freeman 22 jammed, and the boat torpedoed the back of a Seamaster that was waiting below the lock. Such was the scream of the engine, the shouts of the crew and the splintering crash of fibreglass that no-one either heard or saw the crewman hit the water. It was only when the engine had been shut down that his frantic struggle for survival was noticed.

'Help!' he gurgled, as he splashed around the stern of his boat. 'I can't swim! Help!'

The skipper rushed to the stern and tried to reach him with a boathook, but the victim had floated a little way downstream by then and was floundering around beneath a weeping willow.

The lockkeeper materialised on the bull-nose, and looked down on the situation with calm appraisal. Two damaged boats, a lot of people running around and a crewman, without a lifejacket, apparently making a noisy job of drowning. But instead of picking up a lifering and leaping to the rescue, the keeper cupped both hands to his mouth.

'You in the water!' he bellowed. 'Walk!' The crewman's head jerked up. 'I said walk!' The crewman stopped struggling, and tentatively lowered his feet. To everyone's surprise, he stood up in less than four feet of water.

The Bridge

When a small cruiser came into Boveney Lock, the keeper went to help the only person aboard with his ropes. 'No crew today?' he asked conversationally.

'Oh yes,' the man replied, 'I've got my brother and nephew with me.' The keeper looked at the empty boat. Sensing his confusion, the boater smiled weakly, and pointed upriver.

'They're just coming,' he said.

Sure enough, swimming strongly towards the lock, were the two crewmen, both grinning broadly.

'Sorry,' one of them called, 'we fell off the layby. We couldn't climb back up the riverbank, so can we use your steps, please?'

Four entertaining ways to fall in

Jumping a five foot gap whilst holding a four foot rope

Walking backwards down a stairwell

Playing piggy in the middle

Stepping back on board a boat that has already gone without you

A hireboat came weaving down Romney lock-cut with her crew busily getting her ready for the lock ahead. On the bow a lanky young man was carefully coiling a rope, and so intent was he on his task that he didn't notice the helmsman inexplicably steering hard to starboard. Next moment, the boat crashed heavily into the offshore layby and the unsuspecting crewman was launched into space. As he crawled ashore, soaked to the skin and spattered with mud, his skipper left the controls and regarded him stonily with hands on hips.

'Honestly, Roger,' he exploded, 'you bloody exhibitionist!'

The Harpoon

9

Hooray for Henley

Boater: 'It's quiet today. Where is everyone?'
Keeper: 'Probably all at the Henley Regatta, sir.'
Boater: 'Really. And where is that being held, then?'
Keeper: 'Oh, Henley this year, I think.'

Everyone has heard of the Henley Regatta. As far as the social calendar is concerned, it ranks only second to Royal Ascot as the place to be seen, and people flock in their thousands to eat, drink and be merry - and maybe even watch some of the rowing.

For one week in early July, the meadows that border the Thames at this lovely little town are swamped by a sea of canvas and bunting. Grandstands, marquees, bars and all the paraphernalia of a major international event spread along the riverbank. In the privileged enclosures, wealth and status are unashamedly on display, whilst in the corporate hospitality tents, major deals are struck over Pimms and champagne. Out on the river the course is marked out by a long line of temporary white piles, and the cost of a mooring (that's if you can find one) leaps up by 1000%.

Caught up in the middle of all this is the Water Authority. Every year, volunteers are recruited from the lock staff to man the fleet of sleek blue patrol boats. They work alongside the police, plying up and down the reach, rescuing the occasional drunken splasher, preventing collisions and generally keeping an eye on things. Predictably, they are kept quite busy.

One quite important thing they're checking for is the overloading of cruisers. Under the Department of Transport regulations, no motor vessel is allowed to carry more than twelve persons on board unless it is especially licensed to do so. At Henley, where everything that floats is crammed with people, this regulation is often ignored, and skippers become indignant when asked to disembark a considerable excess of bodies. 'They're crew!' the skipper will grumble. 'They're exempt.'

The inspector merely smiles. 'All ten of them, sir?'

'Well, she's a big boat...'

The Regatta is a good chance to show off your rowing skills

A student borrowed his father's canalboat for the Regatta, and invited some university friends to join him. They in turn invited their friends, and the student ended up with 27 people on board. As it was a gloriously sunny day, they all sat on the topsides and broke out the drink.

Dangerously overloaded, the little canalboat chugged along the reach, her passengers laughing and absorbing sunshine and alcohol in roughly equal proportions. What the young man hadn't realised was that the engine was of the air-cooled variety, with a large slot in the hull acting as a ventilator. Due to the excessive weight on the roof, this slot was now barely an inch above the water. A disaster was inevitable, and not long in coming.

A large cruiser swept by too fast and too close, and her wash slammed against the hull. Before anyone knew what had happened, the canalboat was sinking. One minute she was solidly afloat, and the next she had sat down at the stern and slid beneath the surface, leaving 27 expensively-dressed revellers flapping around in the water. Fortunately, no-one was inside the boat when it sank, and the 'crew' were all able to swim to safety. But the student had the uncomfortable task of telling his father that the reason the boat wasn't at the bottom of the garden was because it was actually at the bottom of the river.

A reveller in one of the privileged enclosures was heard to exclaim, 'To hell with the rowing, lets get on with the Regatta!'
He wasn't the only one to comment on the social rather than the sporting aspect of the event. Another gentleman, resplendent in blazer, boater, snow-white trousers and cravat, was most upset to see another well-dressed reveller in the exclusive Stewards' Enclosure. 'He's no right to be in here,' he cried. 'That man's my plumber!'

Out on the river, one of the steamers had been hired for the week by a well-known company. It had cost them £16,000, and they were lavishing champagne and corporate hospitality on their international customers. As the steamer cruised slowly past the starting line, one of the guests asked the waiter if he had a programme.

'A programme, sir?' replied the waiter. 'What for?'

Once the final races have been run and the various winners awarded their trophies by a distinguished VIP, a mammoth firework display marks the end of the Regatta for another year. After the last window-rattling detonation there follows a mass exodus of thousands of revellers. Many jump into their cars and drive straight into the arms of the police, waiting patiently by the exits with breathalisers.

There is no drink-drive ban afloat, however, which is just as well because hundreds of cruisers with their intoxicated crews will turn east or west and begin weaving their way home. The two small locks that enclose the reach, Marsh and Hambledon, are specially floodlit, and remain manned until 2am because there is usually someone who needs fishing out.

Not everyone joins in this mad rush home after the fireworks. Quite a few cruisers remain moored beside the meadows until the following morning, and it was one of these which played host to the weary crew of a patrol boat that had just finished work for the day. As the patrol boat lay snugly alongside, the cruiser owner plied the inspector and boatmen with hospitality until they were in no fit state to leave. 'Stay the night,' he suggested. 'Plenty of room! You can get the boat back early tomorrow.'

They gratefully accepted his offer and the next morning, nursing inevitable hangovers, they crawled out on deck and lowered themselves gingerly into their boat. After the hustle and bustle of the night before, the river was eerily silent. The reach was shrouded in a thick white mist which hid everything except the tops of the trees. The engine was started, the patrol boat left the side of the cruiser, and after a few hundred yards she crashed bodily into the back of a large motoryacht moored off a jetty.

No-one was really to blame. The white hull in the white mist had been almost invisible, and there had been no time to avoid a collision.

The inspector groaned, and asked the boatman to go alongside

to make their apologies. To do this, the patrol boat first had to back off into the mist again. Just as she was swallowed up, the rear door of the cruiser flew open and the pyjama-clad owner stumbled out on deck, unshaven, bleary-eyed and looking for the culprit. A few seconds later the patrol boat emerged from the mist again, and was immediately hailed by the irate owner.

'Hey you!' he cried. 'Come here.' As the boat nudged alongside, the inspector received a barrage from the owner.

'Some bloody imbecile just rammed my boat!' he stormed. 'Did you see him?'

The inspector blinked. 'Are you, er, damaged at all?' he ventured.

'Not a ruddy scratch. But that's not the point. He damn near tipped me out of bed!'

The inspector silently thanked the rubber protective strip that surrounded his boat, and then turned his attention to diplomacy. In this case, he decided, discretion was the better part of valour.

'We've had a lot of complaints about this character this morning,' he said, with a solemn expression. 'That's why we're out looking for him now. But don't you worry. If we catch him, we'll have his guts for garters!'

10

Winter

I saw three ships come sailing by,
On Christmas day, on Christmas day,
And who do you think was in those ships,
On Christmas day, on Christmas day,
It was old Joe Bloggs and his family,
On Christmas day, on Christmas day,
'We thought we'd give you something to do',
On Christmas day, on Christmas day,
I said 'There's always one like you',
On Christmas day, on Christmas day,
'Remember I knock off at four',
On Christmas day, on Christmas day,
He said 'If I'm late I'll rap on your door',
On Christmas day, on Christmas day,
I said,'If you do, you'll get what for!'
On Christmas day in the morning.

George Fielder

Unlike spring, with its opening onslaught at Easter, there is no official end to the boating season. The traffic on the waterways just slowly peters out until eventually a whole day can go by without a single customer. On the coastal marinas there is still a small hard-core of traffic during the week: local fishermen, boat delivery skippers, sailing schools and some die-hard cruising folk who don't seem to mind the freezing cold, the grey clouds and the short hours of daylight.

With so little traffic around, the winter is a good time to repair

97

anything which has suffered during the summer. The various guardians of the waterways start replacing gates, piles and camp-shedding, and publish a list of lock closures for the few customers who might be interested.

One of the lock staff went off on a busman's holiday at the end of the season, chugging up the Oxford Canal in his steel narrowboat. He had carefully checked the stoppages beforehand, but halfway up he came across an emergency lock closure. He moored up just below it, intending to retrace his steps the following day.

During the night there was a violent gale, and in the cold light of day the keeper saw he wasn't going to go anywhere. A massive oak tree had fallen across the canal behind him, completely cutting him off. With the British Waterways workmen stretched to the limit, the poor fellow spent his entire week's holiday trapped in a 100-yard stretch of canal.

Boater's wife in summer... *...and in winter*

How to keep a bollard warm

During the winter, the keepers have to carefully tend their weirs. The water levels rise with seasonal rainfall, and constant adjustments are needed. During a foul, windswept day a young keeper lost his footing whilst trying to clear some wreckage, and tumbled into the swirling water of the weir pool. His automatic lifejacket (a compulsory item when working alone over the water) inflated with a roar, and the current bore him swiftly downstream.

About a mile below the weir was a marina, and the frozen young man was swept against one of the boats moored to the bank. By good fortune the owners were on board doing some maintenance, and heard the dull thud of his impact against the hull. An elderly woman peered out through the canopy and saw the sodden figure hanging on to a fender, wide-eyed and with his teeth chattering in the cold. 'Oh, come and look dear!' she called into the cabin. 'I do believe it's the lockkeeper!'

'I see the ice is a bit thicker this year.'

For most of the lock staff, however, winter is usually a lonely and desolate time, especially on the more remote parts of the manned waterways. If you happen to be out cruising, expect to be waylaid for a chat by a lockkeeper who will be glad to see another human being.

Many is the time the phone will ring, and an invitation be extended from a colleague. 'We're all meeting for a Christmas drink. Come along.'

Over a pint of beer in an oak-beamed pub, and with a real log fire roaring away in the hearth, the lock staff from a stretch of river will gather round a table and reminisce about their summer. It is to their recollections, and the thousands of boaters who bounced merrily through my lock, that I owe this book.

Fortunately, the season of solitude doesn't last long. Come Easter time, the cruisers will be back, hanging, crashing and splashing as never before, but until then I'll leave you with an interesting thought from a woman who was out walking her dog on the towpath.

'It certainly is raw today,' she told the relief lockkeeper, pulling her scarf more firmly around her neck. 'Tell me, if the river freezes over, can you all go home?'

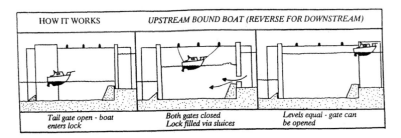

HOW IT WORKS	UPSTREAM BOUND BOAT (REVERSE FOR DOWNSTREAM)

Tail gate open - boat enters lock

Both gates closed Lock filled via sluices

Levels equal - gate can be opened

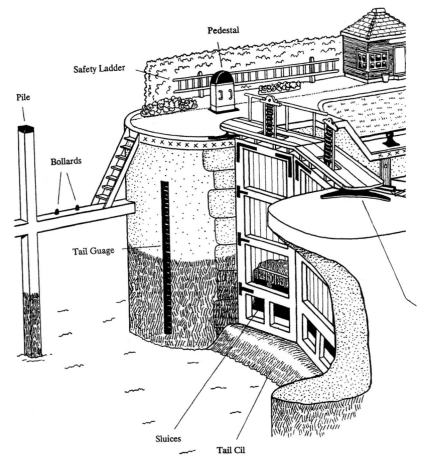

Pedestal

Safety Ladder

Pile

Bollards

Tail Guage

Sluices

Tail Cil

A SIMPLIFIED CUTAWAY DIAGRAM OF AN

ELECTRO-HYDRAULIC LOCK

on the

RIVER THAMES

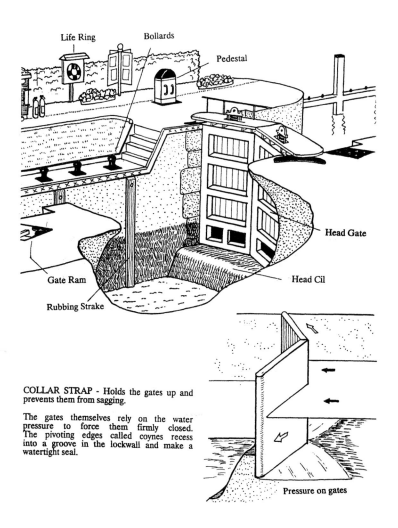

Life Ring

Bollards

Pedestal

Head Gate

Head Cil

Gate Ram

Rubbing Strake

COLLAR STRAP - Holds the gates up and prevents them from sagging.

The gates themselves rely on the water pressure to force them firmly closed. The pivoting edges called coynes recess into a groove in the lockwall and make a watertight seal.

Pressure on gates

Nothing should interrupt a good read!

Don't miss your copy